the center for
hermeneutical
studies

in HELLENISTIC and MODERN CULTURE

The GRADUATE THEOLOGICAL UNION & The UNIVERSITY of CALIFORNIA

BERKELEY, CALIFORNIA

colloquy
27

Editor   Wilhelm Wuellner
                                Pacific School of Religion
                                1798 Scenic Avenue
                                Berkeley, California 94709, U.S.A.

Executive Committee of the Center for Hermeneutical Studies for 1976/1977:

Julian Boyd   University of California, Berkeley
                                English
Gerard E. Caspary   University of California, Berkeley
                                History
Edward C. Hobbs   Graduate Theological Union, Berkeley
                                Theology and Hermeneutics of the New Testament
Thomas G. Rosenmeyer   University of California, Berkeley
                                Greek and Comparative Literature
David Winston   Graduate Theological Union, Berkeley
                                Hellenistic and Judaic Studies
Wilhelm Wuellner   Graduate Theological Union, Berkeley
                                New Testament

The Center for Hermeneutical Studies arose as a response to growing awareness of the fragmentation and the lack of direction in humanistic research, specifically in the area of Hellenistic studies, post-Biblical Judaica, and studies in early Christianity.

In the belief that (1) team effort is essential for real growth in these fields, and that (2) methodological breakthroughs will likely occur where scholars of a variety of fields encounter each other seriously in pursuit of common interests, a group of New Testament scholars at the Graduate Theological Union in Berkeley formed the Center for Hermeneutical Studies in Hellenistic and Modern Culture, during the Spring of 1969. The next step was the creation of a network of relationships and cooperation between scholars of the Graduate Theological Union and those in various fields within the University of California who share their interests in Hellenistic studies and in the problems of hermeneutics involved in their significance for modern culture.

The Center brings together faculty members of the departments of Classics, Comparative Literature, English, Folklore, History, Law, Near Eastern Studies, Rhetoric, and others at the University of California, and from the Graduate Theological Union including the Center for Judaic Studies, as well as select graduate students from each institution, and from other universities and research institutes.

Besides monthly or quarterly colloquies, published in the Protocol Series of the Center, the Executive Committee of the Center organizes and schedules Task Force Work Projects and Research Seminars.

the CENTER for
hermeneutical
studies

in H E L L E N I S T I C and M O D E R N C U L T U R E

The GRADUATE THEOLOGICAL UNION & The UNIVERSITY of CALIFORNIA

BERKELEY, CALIFORNIA

PROTOCOL OF THE TWENTY-SEVENTH COLLOQUY: 13 FEBRUARY 1977

HERMENEUTIC OF THE IDEA OF REVELATION

PAUL RICOEUR, PROFESSOR OF PHILOSOPHY

UNIVERSITY OF PARIS   UNIVERSITY OF CHICAGO

W. WUELLNER, Editor

ISSN   0098-0900

Key title:
Protocol of the colloquy of the Center for Hermeneutical Studies
in Hellenistic and Modern Culture

Library of Congress Cataloging in Publication Data

Center for Hermeneutical Studies in Hellenistic and
    Modern Culture.
    Hermeneutic of the idea of revelation.

    (Protocol series of the colloquies of the Center
for Hermeneutical Studies in Hellenistic and Modern
Culture ; no. 27 ISSN 0089-0900)
    Includes bibliographical references.
    1. Bible-Hermeneutics--Congresses.
2. Hermeneutics--Congresses. 3. Revelation--
Biblical teaching--Congresses. I. Ricoeur, Paul.
II. Title. III. Series: Center for Hermeneutical
Studies in Hellenistic and Modern Culture. Protocol
series of the colloquies ; no. 27.
BS476.C43 1977   220.6'3   77-10157
ISBN 0-89242-026-X

Published by

The Center for Hermeneutical Studies in
Hellenistic and Modern Culture

2465 Le Conte Avenue
Berkeley, CA 94709, USA

TABLE OF CONTENTS

HERMENEUTIC OF THE IDEA OF REVELATION

PAUL RICOEUR

The question of revelation is a formidable one in the proper sense of the word, not only because it may be seen as the first and the last question for faith, but also because it has been obscured by so many false debates that the recovery of a real question in itself constitutes an enormous task. My paper is devoted to just this enterprise.

The way of posing the question which, more than any other, I will seek to overcome is the one that sets in opposition an authoritarian and opaque concept of revelation and a concept of reason which claims to be its own master and transparent to itself. This is why my presentation will be a battle on two fronts: it seeks to recover a concept of revelation and a concept of reason which, without ever coinciding, can at least enter into a living dialectic and together engender something like an understanding of faith.

I. The Primary Expressions of Revelation

I will begin on the side of revelation, and my first remarks will be devoted to rectifying the concept of revelation so that we may get beyond what I have called the accepted opaque and authoritarian understanding of this concept.

By an opaque concept of revelation, I mean that familiar amalgamation of three levels of language in one form of traditional teaching about revelation: first, the level of the confession of faith where the *lex credendi* is not separated from the *lex orandi*; second, the level of ecclesial dogma where a historic community interprets for itself and for others the understanding of faith specific to its tradition; and third, the body of doctrines imposed by the magisterium as the rule of orthodoxy. The particular amalgamation that I deplore and that I am seeking to combat is always made in terms of the third level, which is why it is not merely opaque, but also authoritarian.

I do not intend to deny the specificity of the work of formulating dogma, whether at the ecclesial level or at the level of theological investigation. But I do affirm its derived and subordinate character. This is why I will endeavor to carry the notion of revelation back to its most primary level, the one which (for the sake of brevity) I call the discourse of faith or the confession of faith.

In what manner is the category of revelation included in this discourse? This question seems all the more legitimate to me in that, on the one hand, the philosopher cannot discover or learn much from a level of discourse organized in terms of philosophy's own speculative categories, for he then discovers fragments borrowed from his own discourse and the travesty of this discourse that results from its authoritarian and opaque use. On the other hand, he may discover and learn much from nonspeculative discourse--what Whitehead called barbaric discourse because it had not yet been illuminated by the philosophical logos. What is more, it is a long-held conviction of mine that the philosopher's opposite in this type of debate is not the theologian, but the believer who is informed by the exegete; I mean, the believer who seeks to understand himself through a better understanding of the texts of his faith.

The principal benefit of such a return to the origin of theological discourse is that from the outset it places reflection before a variety of expressions of faith, all modulated by the varieties of discourse within which the faith of Israel and later of the early church is set down. So instead of having to confront a monolithic concept of revelation, which is only obtained by transforming these different forms of discourse into propositions, we encounter a concept of revelation which is pluralistic, polysemic, and at most analogical in form--the very term revelation, as we shall see, being borrowed from one of these forms of discourse.

1. _Prophetic Discourse_. Which of the biblical forms of discourse should be taken as the basic referent for a meditation on the idea of revelation? It seems legitimate to begin by taking prophetic discourse as our basic axis of inquiry. Indeed, this is the discourse which declares itself to be pronounced in the name of ..., and exegetes have rightly pointed out the importance of its introductory formula: "The word of Yahweh came to me, saying, 'Go and proclaim in the hearing of Jerusalem,...'" (Jeremiah 2:1). Here is the original nucleus of the traditional idea of revelation. The prophet presents himself as not speaking in his own name, but in the name of another, in the name of Yahweh. So here the idea of revelation appears as identified with the idea of a double author of speech and writing. Revelation is the speech of another behind the speech of the prophet.

Yet if we separate the prophetic mode of discourse from its context, and especially if we separate it from that narrative discourse which is so important for constituting Israel's faith, as well as the faith of the early church, we risk imprisoning the idea of revelation in too narrow a concept, the concept of the speech of another. When extended to all the other forms of discourse from the Old Testament we are going to consider, this concept of revelation, taken as a synonym for revelation in general, leads to the idea of scripture as dictated, as something whispered in someone's ear. The idea of revelation is then confused with the idea of a double author of sacred texts, and any access to a less subjective manner of understanding revelation is prematurely cut off. In turn, the very idea of inspiration, as arising from meditation on the Holy Spirit, is deprived of the enrichment it might receive from those forms of discourse which are less easily interpreted in terms of a voice behind a voice or of a double author of scripture.

2. _Narrative Discourse_. For these reasons, we must not limit ourselves to simply identifying revelation with prophecy. The other modes of discourse bear this out. To see this, we need surely to begin by considering the narrative genre of discourse that dominates the Pentateuch, as well as the synoptic Gospels and the Book of Acts.

What does revelation mean as regards these texts? Should we say that as with the prophetic texts, these texts have a double author, the writer and the spirit which guides him? Should we really attend above all else to the question of the narrator? Theoreticians of narrative discourse have noted that in narration the author often disappears and it is as though the events recounted themselves. This insight suggests that we should pay more attention to the things recounted than to the narrator and his prompter. Let us follow this trail. Where does it lead? Essentially to meditation on the character of the events recounted, including the election of Abraham, the Exodus, the anointing of David, etc. in the Old Testament, and the resurrection of Christ for the early church. The idea of revelation then appears as connected to the very character of these events. What is noteworthy about them is that they do not simply occur and then pass away. They mark an epoch and engender history. In this vein, the Jewish scholar Emil Fackenheim is correct when he speaks of "history-making events." These events found an epoch because they have the twofold characteristic of both founding a community and of delivering it from a great danger, which, moreover, may take diverse forms. In such instances, to speak of revelation is to qualify the events in question as transcendent in relation to the ordinary course of history.

What is essential in the case of narrative discourse, therefore, is the emphasis on the founding event or events as the imprint, mark, or trace of God's act. Confession takes place through narration and the problematic of inspiration is in no way the primary consideration. God's mark is in history before being in speech. It is only secondarily in speech inasmuch as this history itself is brought to language in the speech-act of narration.

To recognize the specificity of this form of discourse, therefore, is to guard ourselves against a certain narrowness of any theology of the word which only attends to word-events. In the encounter with what we could call the idealism of the theology of the word-event, we must reaffirm the realism of the event of history--as is indicated today by the work of a theologian such as Wolfhart Pannenberg in his attempts to rectify the one-sided emphasis of Fuchs and Ebeling.

Then, too, narration includes prophecy in its domain to the extent that prophecy is narrative in its style. Indeed, the meaning of prophecy is not exhausted by the subjectivity of the prophet. Prophecy is carried forward toward the "Day of Yahweh," which the prophet says will not be a day of joy, but of terror. This term, the Day of Yahweh, announces something like an event which will be to impending history what the founding events were to the history recounted in the great biblical narratives.

There is also, however, a tension between narration and prophecy at the level of the event. In the dialectic of the prophetic event, the same history which narration founds as certain is suddenly undercut by the menace announced in the prophecy. The supporting pedestal totters. It is the structure of history which is at stake here, not merely the quality of the word which pronounces it. And revelation is implicated in this now narrative, now prophetic understanding of history.

But the polysemy and polyphony of revelation are not yet exhausted by this coupling of narration and prophecy, for there are at least three other modes of religious discourse in the Old Testament which are not included within this polarity of narration and prophecy. The first of these is the Torah, or instruction, conveyed to Israel.

3. Prescriptive Discourse. Broadly speaking, we may call this aspect of revelation its practical dimension. It corresponds to the symbolic expression "the will of God." But this idea of revelation in the form of instruction is in turn full of pitfalls for the traditional understanding of revelation. In this regard, the translation of the word Torah by νόμος or

"law" beginning with the Septuagint is completely misleading. It leads us, in effect, to enclose the idea of an imperative from above within the idea of a divine law. The idea of dependence is essential to the idea of revelation, as I will indicate in the second part of this paper, but to really understand this primary dependence within the orders of speaking, willing, and being, we must first criticize the ideas of heteronomy and autonomy, both as taken together and as symmetrical to each other.

Let us concentrate for the moment on the idea of heteronomy. Nothing is more inadequate than this idea for making sense of what the term Torah has signified within Jewish experience. Three points are worth emphasizing.

First, it is not unimportant that the legislative texts of the Old Testament are placed in the mouth of Moses and within the narrative framework of the sojourn at Sinai. This means that this instruction is organically connected to the founding events symbolized by the exodus from Egypt. And in this regard, the introductory formula of the Decalogue constitutes an essential link connecting the story of the Exodus and the proclamation of the Law: "I am Yahweh, your God, who brought you out of the land of Egypt, out of the house of bondage" (Ex. 20:2). It signifies that the memory of deliverance qualifies the instruction in an intimate way. The Decalogue is the Law of a redeemed people. Such an idea is foreign to any simple concept of heteronomy.

This first comment leads to a second. The Law is one aspect of a much more concrete and encompassing relationship than that between commanding and obeying which characterizes the imperative. This relationship is the one that the Covenant itself imperfectly translates, for the idea of the Covenant designates a whole complex of relationships, running from the most fearful and meticulous obedience of the Law to casuistic interpretations, to intelligent meditation, to pondering in the heart, to the veneration of a joyous soul--as we shall see better with regard to the Psalms.

This range of variations opened by the Covenant for our ethical feelings suggests a third reflection. Despite the apparently invariable and apodictic character of the Decalogue, the Torah unfolds within a dynamism which we may characterize as its historical aspect. Without falling into that old rut of opposing the legalistic and the prophetic, we may rediscover in the very teaching of the Torah an unceasing alternation which by turns sets the Law out in endlessly multiplying prescriptions or draws it together by summing it up in one set of commandments which retain only its direction toward holiness. If we fail to recognize this intimate alternation within the Torah, we cannot understand how Jesus could, on the one hand, oppose the "traditions of the elders," and, on the other hand, declare that in the Kingdom the law would be fulfilled to its last iota. In this sense, the Sermon on the Mount proclaims the same intention of perfection and holiness that runs through the ancient Law. And it is this intention which constitutes the ethical dimension of revelation. If we continue to speak of revelation as historical, it is not only in the sense that the trace of God may be read in the founding events of the past or in a coming conclusion to history, but also in the sense that it orients practical history and engenders the dynamics of institutions.

4. <u>Wisdom Discourse</u>. But would this deepening of the Law beyond its being scattered in precepts be perceived clearly if another dimension of revelation was not also recognized in its own specificity? I mean, revelation

as wisdom. Wisdom finds its literary expression in wisdom literature. But wisdom also surpasses every literary genre. At first glance, it appears as the art of living well, expert advice on the way to true happiness. But behind this somewhat shabby facade, we need to discern the great vocation of a reflection on existence which has in view the individual beyond the community of the people of the Covenant, and through him, every man. The counsels of wisdom ignore the frontiers where any legislation appropriate to a single people stops, even if it is the legislation of an elect people. Wisdom has in view every man in and through the Jew. Its themes are those boundary-situations spoken of by Karl Jaspers, those situations--including solitude, guilt, suffering, and death--where the misery and the grandeur of man confront each other. In this way, wisdom fulfills one of religion's fundamental functions which is to bind together *ethos* and *cosmos*, the sphere of human action and the sphere of the world. It does not do this by demonstrating that this conjunction is given in things, nor by demanding that it be produced through our action. Rather it joins *ethos* and *cosmos* at the very point of their discordance: in suffering and, more precisely, in unjust suffering. Wisdom does not teach us how to avoid suffering, or how to magically deny it, or how to dissimulate it under an illusion. It teaches us how to endure, how to suffer suffering.

This is perhaps the profoundest meaning of the Book of Job, the best example of wisdom. Job's questions about justice are undoubtedly left without an answer. But by repenting, though not of sin, for he is righteous, but by repenting for his supposition that existence does not make sense, Job presupposes an unsuspected meaning which no speech or *logos* man may have at his disposal can transcribe. This meaning has no other expression than the new quality penitence confers on his suffering. Hence it is not unrelated to what Aristotle speaks of as the tragic pathos which purifies the spectator of fear and pity.

It should be beginning to be apparent how the notion of revelation differs from one mode of discourse to another; especially when we pass from prophecy to wisdom. The prophet claims divine inspiration as guaranteeing what he says. The sage does nothing of the sort. He does not declare that his speech is the speech of another. But he does know that wisdom precedes him and that in a way it is through participation in wisdom that a man may be said to be wise.

5. <u>Hymnic Discourse</u>. I do not want to end this brief survey of modes of biblical discourse without saying something about the lyric genre best exemplified by the Psalms. Hymns of praise, supplications, and thanksgiving constitute its three major genres. Clearly they are not marginal forms of religious discourse. The praise addressed to God's prodigious accomplishments in nature and history is not a movement of the heart which is added to the narrative genre without any effect on its nucleus. In fact, celebration elevates the story and turns it into an invocation. And in this sense, to recount the story is already a form of celebration. Furthermore, without the supplications in the psalms concerning suffering, would the plaint of the righteous also find the path to invocation, even if it must lead to dispute and recrimination? Through supplication, the righteous man's protestations of innocence have as an opposite a Thou who may respond to his plaint.

This movement toward the second person finds its fulfillment in the psalms of thanksgiving where the uplifted soul thanks someone. Here the invocation reaches its highest purity, its most disinterested expression, when

the supplication unburdened of every demand is converted into recognition.
Thus under the three figures of praise, supplication, and thanksgiving, human
speech becomes invocation. Here it is addressed to God in the second
person, without limiting itself to designating him in the third person as in
narration, or to speaking in the first person in his name as in prophecy.
We must notice therefore that in passing through the three positions of the
system of singular personal pronouns--I, you, he--the origin of revelation is
designated in different modalities which are never completely identical with
one another.

If we were to say in what sense the psalter could be said to be
revealed, it would certainly not be so in the sense that its praise, supplication, and thanksgiving were placed in their disparate authors' mouths by God,
but in the sense that the sentiments expressed there are formed by and conform
to their object. Revelation is this very formation of our feelings which
transcends their daily and ordinary modalities.

If we now look back over the path we have covered, certain important
conclusions are discernible.

First, I will reiterate my original affirmation that the analysis of
religious discourse ought not to begin with the level of theological assertions
such as "God exists," "God is immutable, omnipotent, etc." A hermeneutic of
revelation must give priority to those modalities of discourse that are most
primary within the language of a community of faith. ·

Second, these primary expressions are caught up in forms of discourse
as diverse as narration, prophecy, legislative texts, wisdom sayings, hymns,
supplications, and thanksgiving. One mistaken assumption here would be to take
these forms of discourse as simple literary genres which ought to be
neutralized so that we can extract their theological content. To uproot this
prejudice we must convince ourselves that the literary genres of the Bible do
not constitute a rhetorical facade which it would be possible to pull down
in order to reveal some thought content that is indifferent to its literary
vehicle. The confession of faith expressed in the biblical documents is
directly modulated by the forms of discourse wherein it is expressed. This is
why the difference between story and prophecy, so characteristic of the Old
Testament, is *per se* theologically significant. And the same thing applies to
the Torah, as well as to the spiritual tenor of the hymn. What announces
itself there is in each instance qualified by the form of the announcement.
The religious "saying" is constituted in the interplay between story and
prophecy, history and legislation, legislation and wisdom, and finally wisdom
and lyricism.

Third, if the forms of religious discourse are so pregnant with meaning,
the notion of revelation may no longer be formulated in a uniform and monotonous
fashion which we presuppose when we speak of *the* biblical revelation.
Instead we arrive at a polysemic and polyphonic concept of revelation.

Earlier I spoke of such a concept as analogical. Now I want to explain
this analogy. It proceeds from a reference term: prophetic discourse.
There revelation signifies inspiration from a first person to a first person.
But if we do not see the analogical bond between the other forms of religious

discourse and prophetic discourse we generalize in univocal fashion the concept of inspiration derived from the prophetic genre and assume that God spoke to the redactors of the sacred books just as he spoke to the prophets. The Scriptures are then said to have been written by the Holy Spirit and we are inclined to construct a uniform theology of the double divine and human author where God is posited as the formal cause and the writer is posited as the instrumental cause of these texts.

However, by taking up this generalization, we do not do justice to those traits of revelation that are not reducible to being synonymous with the double voice of the prophet. The narrative genre invited us to displace onto the recounted events that revealing light that proceeds from their founding value and their instituting function. In a similar manner, the nuances of revelation that are derived from the prescriptive force of instruction, the illuminating capacity of the wisdom saying, and the quality of lyrical pathos in the hymn, are connected to these forms of discourse. Inspiration, then, also designates the coming to language of this prescriptive force, this illuminating capacity, and this lyric pathos as analogous to one another.

Allow me now to draw one final consequence which will carry us to the threshold of the philosophical reflection that is to follow. If one thing may be said unequivocally about all the analogical forms of revelation, it is that in none of its modalities may revelation be included in and dominated by knowledge. In this regard the idea of something secret is the limit-idea of revelation. It is, in other words, a twofold idea. The God who reveals himself is a hidden God and hidden things belong to him.

The confession that God is infinitely above man's thoughts and speech, that he guides us without our comprehending his ways, that the fact that man is an enigma to himself even obscures the clarity that God communicates to him--this confession belongs to the idea of revelation. The one who reveals himself is also the one who conceals himself. And in this regard nothing is as significant as the episode of the burning bush in Exodus 3. Tradition has quite rightly named this episode the revelation of the divine name. For this name is precisely unnameable. Moses asked, "If I come to the people of Israel and say to them, 'The God of your fathers has sent me to you,' and they ask me, 'What is his name?' what shall I say to them?" God answered, "I am who I am." And he added, "Say this to the children of Israel, 'I am has sent me to you.'" The appellation Yahweh--he is--is not a name which defines God, but one which signifies, one which signifies the act of deliverance.

To say that the God who reveals himself is a hidden God is to confess that revelation can never constitute a body of truths that an institution may boast of or take pride in possessing. So to dissipate the massive opacity of the concept of revelation is also at the same time to overthrow every totalitarian form of authority which might claim to withhold the revealed truth.

II. The Response of a Hermeneutic Philosophy

What is philosophy's task in response to the claim which proceeds from a concept of revelation as differentiated as the one I have just outlined? Claim--*Anspruch*--can signify two different things: undue and unacceptable pretension, or, an appeal which does not force one to accept its message. I want to understand claim in this second sense. But this reversal in listening to a claim can only be produced if, in symmetry with the critique of an opaque and authoritarian concept of revelation, philosophy proceeds in its own self-understanding to a critique of its own pretension which causes it to understand the appeal of revelation as an unacceptable claim opposed to it. If the unacceptable claim of the idea of revelation is in the final analysis that of a *sacrificium intellectus* and of a total heteronomy under the verdict of the magisterium, the opposed claim of philosophy is the claim to a complete transparency of truth and a total autonomy of the thinking subject. When these two claims simply confront each other, they constitute an unbridgeable canyon between what some call the "truths of faith" and others call the "truths of reason."

I want to direct my remarks to a critique of this double pretension of philosophy, with the idea that at the end of such an undertaking the apparently unreasonable claim of revelation might be better understood as a nonviolent appeal. My analysis will consist of two parts, corresponding to the twofold claim of philosophical discourse to transparent objectivity and subjective autonomy. Indeed, these two dimensions of the problem correspond to the two major objections that are usually directed against the very principle of revelation. According to the first objection, any idea of revelation violates the idea of objective truth as measured by the criteria of empirical verification and falsification. According to the second objection, the idea of revelation denies the autonomy of the thinking subject inscribed within the idea of a consciousness completely in control of itself. The double meditation I propose will address in turn these claims to transparency founded on a concept of truth as correspondence and verification, and to autonomy founded on the concept of a sovereign consciousness.

If I begin with the former point, it is for a fundamental reason, namely that the conquest of a new concept of truth as manifestation—and in this sense as revelation—demands the recognition of man's real dependence which is in no way synonymous with heteronomy.

1. The world of the text and the new being. My first investigation, into what I will call the space of the manifestation of things, takes place within precise limits. I will not speak of our experience of being-in-the-world beginning from a phenomenology of perception as may be found in the works of Husserl and Merleau-Ponty, nor in terms of a phenomenology of care or preoccupation as may be found in Heidegger's *Being and Time*—although I believe that they may be connected by means of the detour I propose. Instead I will begin directly from the manifestation of the world by the text and by scripture.

This approach may seem overly limited due to the fact that it proceeds through the narrow defile of one cultural fact, the existence of written documents, and thus because it is limited to cultures which possess books, but it will seem less limited if we comprehend what enlargement of our experience of the world results from the existence of such documents. Moreover, by choosing this angle of attack, we immediately establish a correspondence with the fact that the claim of revealed speech reaches us today through writings to be interpreted. Those religions which refer back to Abraham—Judaism, Christianity, and Islam—are in their different ways, and they are often very different ways, religions of the book. So it is therefore appropriate, I believe, to inquire into the particular revelatory function attached to certain modalities of scripture which I will place under the title *Poetics*, in a sense

I will explain in a moment. In effect, under the category of poetics, philosophical analysis encounters those traits of revelation which may correspond
with or respond to the nonviolent appeal of biblical revelation.

I have not introduced the category of poetics heretofore. It does not
designate one of the literary genres discussed in the first part of my
presentation, but rather the totality of these genres inasmuch as they
exercise a referential function that differs from the descriptive referential
function of ordinary language and above all of scientific discourse. Hence
I am speaking of the poetic function of discourse and not of a poetic genre or
a mode of poetic discourse. This function, in turn, is defined particularly
in terms of its referential function. What is this referential function?

As a first approximation, we may say that the poetic function points
to the obliterating of the ordinary referential function, at least if we
identify it with the capacity to describe familiar objects of perception or the
objects which science alone determines by means of standards of measurement.
Poetic discourse suspends this descriptive function. It does not directly augment
our knowledge of objects.

From here it is only a short step to saying that in poetry language
turns back on itself. But if we say this we give in too quickly to the
positivist presupposition that empirical knowledge is objective knowledge
because it is verifiable. Too often, we do not notice that we uncritically
accept a certain concept of truth defined as correspondence to real objects
and as submitted to a criterion of empirical verification. That language in its
poetic function abolishes the type of reference characteristic of such
descriptive discourse, and along with it the reign of truth as adequation and
the very definition of truth in terms of verification, is not to be doubted.
The question is whether this suspension or abolition of a referential function
of the first degree is not the negative condition for the liberating of a
more primitive, more primary referential function which may be called a second
order reference only because discourse whose function is descriptive has
usurped the first rank in daily life and has been supported in this regard by
modern science.

My deepest conviction is that poetic language alone restores to us
that participation-in or belonging-to an order of things which precedes our
capacity to oppose ourselves to things taken as objects opposed to a subject.
Hence one function of poetic discourse is to bring about this emergence of a
depth-structure of belonging-to amid the ruins of descriptive discourse.
And in this regard, the most extreme paradox is that when language most enters
into fiction--for example, when a poet forges the plot of a tragedy--it most
speaks truth because it redescribes reality so well known that it is taken for
granted in terms of the new features of the plot. Fiction and redescription,
then, go hand in hand. Or, to speak like Aristotle in his *Poetics*, the *mythos*
is the way to true *mimesis*, which is not slavish imitation, or a copy or
mirror-image, but a transposition or metamorphosis--or, as I suggested, a redescription.

This conjunction of fiction and redescription, of *mythos* and *mimesis*,
constitutes the referential function by means of which I would define the poetic
dimension of language.

In turn, this poetic function conceals a dimension of revelation where revelation is to be understood in a nonreligious and nontheistic sense, but a sense capable of entering into resonance with one or the other of the aspects of biblical revelation. It is revelatory because the poetic function incarnates a concept of truth that escapes the definition by correspondence as well as the criteria of falsification and verification. Here truth no longer means verification, but manifestation; that is, letting what shows itself be. What shows itself is in each instance a proposed world, a world I may inhabit and wherein I can project my ownmost possibilities. It is in this sense of manifestation that language in its poetic function is a vehicle of revelation.

By using the word revelation in such a nonbiblical and even non-religious way, do we abuse the word? I do not think so. Our analysis of the biblical concept of revelation has prepared us for a first degree analogical use of the term and here we are led to a second degree analogy. This new analogy invites us to place the primary expressions of biblical faith under the sign of the poetic function of language.—Not to deprive them of any referent, but to put them under the law of split reference that characterizes the poetic function.

Finally, just as the world of poetic texts clears a way for itself through the ruins of the intraworldly objects of everyday reality and of science, so the new being projected by the biblical text clears a way through the world of ordinary experience and in spite of the closed nature of that experience. The power to project this new world is the power of breaking through and of an opening.

This non-religious or perhaps a-religious sense of revelation assists us in restoring the concept of biblical revelation to its full dignity. It delivers us from psychologizing interpretations of the inspiration of the scriptures in the sense of an insufflation of their words into the writers' ears. If the Bible may be said to be revealed this must refer to what it says, to the new being it unfolds before us. Revelation, in short, is a feature of the biblical world proposed by the text.

Yet if this a-religious sense of revelation has such a corrective value, it does not for all that include the religious meaning of revelation. There is an analogy between them, but nothing allows us to derive the specific feature of religious language-- that is, that its referent moves among prophecy, narration, prescription, wisdom, and psalms, coordinating these diverse and partial forms of discourse by giving them a vanishing point and an index of incompleteness--nothing, I say, allows us to derive this from the general characteristics of the poetic function. There is an analogy, but it is para-doxical because it is established by the category of the world of the text which mediates between revelation in the broad sense of poetic discourse and in the specifically biblical sense.

2. <u>Mediating reflection and testimony</u>. Let us now turn to philosophy's second pretension that is opposed to the idea of revealed truth. This is its claim to autonomy. It is founded on the concept of a subject who is in charge of his thoughts. This idea of a consciousness which posits itself in positing its contents undoubtedly constitutes the strongest resistance to any idea of revelation, not only in the specific sense of the religions of the book, but also in the larger, more global sense that we have just connected to the poetic function of discourse.

I will proceed here with regard to the second part of my analysis in the same manner as for the first part. That is, instead of taking up the question of the autonomy of consciousness in its most general sense, I will attempt to focus the debate on a central concept of self-awareness that is capable of corresponding to one of the major traits of the idea of revelation brought to light by our analysis of biblical discourse, and this central category will occupy a place comparable to that of poetic discourse in relation to the objective aspect of philosophical discourse. The category which to me best signifies the self-implication of the subject in his discourse is that of *testimony*. Besides having a corresponding term on the side of the idea of revelation, it is the most appropriate concept for making us understand what a thinking subject formed by and conforming to poetic discourse might be.

Few philosophers, to my knowledge, have attempted to integrate the category of testimony into philosophical reflection. Most have either ignored it or abandoned it to the realm of faith. One exception is Jean Nabert in his volume entitled *Désir de Dieu*. I want to draw on this work to show how this category governs the abandonment of or letting go of the absolute claim to self-consciousness, and how it occupies on the subjective side of a hermeneutic of revelation a strategic position similar to that of the category of poetics on the objective side.

Recourse to testimony occurs in a philosophy of reflection at the moment when such a philosophy renounces the pretension of consciousness to constitute itself. Thus Jean Nabert, for example, recognizes the place of testimony at that point of his itinerary where concrete reflection exerts itself to rejoin what he calls that primary affirmation of my existence which constitutes me more than I constitute it. For a philosophy of reflection, this primary affirmation is in no way one of our experiences. It is rather the letting go of all claims to completely master ourselves. Consequently, this letting go takes up from and continues the Kantian meditation on the transcendental illusion as presented in the section on "Dialectic" in the first *Critique*. It might also be expressed by the language of the *Enneads* where Plotinus writes "ἀφέλε πάντα--abolish everything." It is precisely this movement of letting go which bears reflection to the encounter with contingent signs of the absolute which the absolute in its generosity allows to appear.

This avowal of the absolute can no longer be Kantian (nor no doubt Plotinian), for Kantianism inclines us to look only for examples or symbols, not for testimonies, understood as accounts of an experience of the absolute. In an example, the case is effaced before the rule and the person is effaced before the law. An abstraction, the abstraction of the norm, takes the place of the primary affirmation. But the encounter with evil in the experience of what cannot be justified does not allow us the leisure to grant our veneration to the sublimity of the moral order. The unjustifiable constrains us to let go of this very veneration. Only those events, acts, and persons that attest that the unjustifiable is overcome here and now can reopen the path toward primary affirmation.

As for the symbol, it is no less feeble than the example with regard to the unjustifiable. Its inexhaustible richness of meaning no doubt gives it a consistency that the example lacks. But its historicity places it at the mercy of the work of interpretation that may dissipate it too quickly into too-ideal forms of significations. As Nabert says, only "testimony that is singular in each instance confers the sanction of reality on ideas, ideals, and ways of being that the symbol depicts to us and which we uncover as our ownmost possibilities" (*op. cit.* p.37).

Therefore testimony, better than either an example or a symbol, places reflection before the paradox which the pretension of consciousness makes a scandal of; I mean that a moment of history is invested with an absolute character. This paradox ceases to be a scandal as soon as the wholly internal movement of letting go, of abandoning the claim to found consciousness, accepts being led by and ruled by the interpretation of external signs which the absolute gives of itself. And the hermeneutic of testimony consists wholly in the convergence of these two movements, these two exegeses: the exegesis of self and the exegesis of external signs.

Testimony, on the one hand, is able to be taken up internally in reflection thanks to a dialectical feature that arouses and calls for this reflective repetition in us. Indeed, testimony calls for an interpretation through the dialectic of the witness and the things seen. To be a witness is to have participated in what one has seen and to be able to testify to it.

On the other hand, testimony may break away from the things seen to such a degree that it is concentrated on the quality of an act, a work, or a life, which is in itself a sign of the absolute. In this second sense, which is complementary to the first sense, to be a witness is no longer to testify that ..., but to testify to .... This latter expression allows us to understand that a witness may so implicate himself in his testimony that it becomes the best proof of his conviction.

But when this proof becomes the price of life itself, the witness changes names. He becomes a martyr. In Greek, though, μάρτυς (μαρτυρέω) means "to testify." I am well aware that any argument from martyrdom is suspect. A cause that has martyrs is not necessarily a just cause. But martyrdom precisely is not an argument and still less a proof. A person becomes a martyr because first of all he is a witness.

Furthermore, this proximity between a witness and a martyr is not always without effect on the very meaning of testimony. Its purely juridical sense may rise and fall. In a trial, for example, a witness enjoys immunity. Only the accused risks his life. But a witness can become the accused and the righteous may die. Then a great historical archetype arises: the suffering servant, the persecuted righteous man, Socrates, Jesus, ... The commitment or risk assumed by the witness makes testimony more than and other than a simple narration of what was seen. Testimony is also the commitment of a pure heart and a commitment unto death. It thus belongs to the tragic destiny of truth.

This tragic destiny of truth outside of us in a wholly contingent history may accompany the letting go by means of which reflection abandons the illusions of a sovereign consciousness. Reflection does so by internalizing the dialectic of testimony from which it records the trace of the absolute in the contingency of history.

The witness to things seen, we have said, at the limit becomes a martyr for truth. Here reflection must confess its inequality with the historical paradigm of its movement of letting go if it is not to abuse its words and become radically deceitful. The philosophy of reflection tends to use big words: epoché, reflective distance, letting go, etc. But in its use of them it indicates more than it can signify of the direction of a movement, that movement which we have simply wanted to point to with the expression "letting go" as the abandonment of the sovereign consciousness. Philosophy must internalize what is said in the Gospel: "Whoever would save his life must lose it." Transposed into the realm of reflection, this means, "Whoever would posit himself as a constituting consciousness will miss his destiny." But reflection cannot produce this renouncing of the sovereign consciousness out of itself. It may only do so by confessing its total dependence on the historical manifestations of the divine. This is the non-heteronomous dependence of conscious reflection on external testimonies. And it is this dependence that gives philosophy a certain idea of revelation. As earlier with regard to poetic discourse on the objective side of the idea of revelation, so too on the subjective side, the experience of testimony can only provide the horizon for a specifically religious and biblical idea of revelation, without our ever being able to derive that experience from the purely philosophical categories of truth as manifestation and reflection as testimony.

14

Response by Dr. Julian Boyd, Professor of English
University of California, Berkeley

Anglo-American speech-act theory is still unintentionally tied to the deictic model of the three-personal pronoun (not to mention a very similar adverbial over-simplification of place and time).

Following Ricoeur, glimpses, at least, of a paradigm both comforting and alarming can be imaginatively revealed.

If we simply pretend to remove the here/there, now/then, self/non-self, dimension along with the more easily dispensed with distinction of the vocative, which leaves discourse no longer necessarily addressed by or to someone or thing (including even the self to itself), we will have gone one step farther than the narrative theorist's picture mentioned in Ricoeur in which events somehow report themselves. But that is truly pseudo-objective and a really apodeictic view of third person events.

Ricoeur rightly objects along similar lines, I believe, to the command/ obey modality. There is the identical unnecessary deixis involved. Unveiling in this case is no harder to imagine: it is something like an unqualified, but no longer imperative-performative expression of what looks like an "objective" Desire.

This, to me, as a thought-experiment is the nearest thing like faith I can feel.

Response by Dr. Edward C. Hobbs, Professor of Theology and Hermeneutics
Graduate Theological Union, Berkeley

The overall response which I must make to Paul Ricoeur's paper on
Revelation is one of delight that a great philosopher can and does take
seriously a category of marked importance to theologians, as well as pleasure
in observing a superb mind at work probing for new paths through an old
jungle. For he has brought new life to the task attempted in earlier genera-
tions by such thinkers as Augustine and Aquinas: to bring the work of the
philosopher and the work of the theologian into living dialogue with each other.
My overall satisfaction with the paper, and the extent to which I have learned
deeply from it, should be the context within which my critique is interpreted.

I

Ricoeur's emphasis on the primacy of *event* in his discussion of
"Narrative discourse" is a healthy one; it is the emphasis brought to the fore
by the great historical-critical movement of the late nineteenth and early
twentieth centuries. Indeed, "God's mark is in history before being in
speech." But then I am impelled to ask whether in fact such an insight is
reflected by his paper as a whole. Would we not need to concern ourselves
with *historical* analysis, and not just *literary* analysis, of the materials? If
in reality revelation is in *history* before being in speech, then the
revelation is in *events*: not in the events-as-narrated (for this would be
speech, not *history*), but in the events-as-occurring. And this is not altered
by the fact that events-as-occurring are not directly accessible to us, that
they are narrated in various (and incompatible) ways, that only in speech can
we approach them, and so on. If the distinction between history-as-event and
history-as-narration is made at all, we cannot shrink from the problems thereby
posed.

But the moment we make this distinction, and emphasize history as
primary for revelation rather than the narrative of it, we are bound to
discover that much is narrated in the texts concerning events which are not
deemed (in the narrative) to be revelatory in any important way. The long
chapters giving the count of the tribes in the census, the cities captured and
those not vanquished in the invasion of Canaan, the exploits (and sexploits)
of the judges and kings, the petty details of royal family history (and
gossip), the elaborate justification of the Davidic dynasty's claim to
legitimacy, and so on, are not oddities--they constitute a large bulk of our
"narrative discourse." Now, is this revelation? Or is only some of it?
Or do we look for something which distinguishes between some events and others?
That is to say, a *Sachkritik* is necessary (whether it be acknowledged openly,
or--as more usually--sneaked in surreptitiously) to sort out events from events,
or dimensions/aspects of events from other dimensions/aspects.

Now, if the non-propositional character of revelation (at least in
these narrative materials) is recognized, in favor of its event-character first
of all, then we are led by the texts themselves to perceive certain events as
dominating the other materials and as overshadowing (or giving meaning to) other
events. In the case of the Old Testament, this is the Exodus-event; in the
case of the New Testament, the Jesus-event.

This recognition and this perception move us to again make a distinction
made long ago: between *canon* and *revelation*. If all of the materials in the

Bible are taken to be revelation, then the task of sorting out the meaning of revelation is not the same as if all of the materials are taken to be *canon* (i.e., yardstick) of the *meaning* of revelation. Paul, for example, plainly says at one moment, "The Lord says this," and at a later moment, "I say this, not the Lord, though I think I have his mind." If *Jesus* is understood as revelation, not the Gospels, then we can cope with four quite different Gospels as different *but legitimate* interpretations, all within (not outside) the limits of right interpretation of the event (i.e., within the canon). But if the *Gospels* are taken as the revelation, then we will be driven to harmonize (by whatever means) the conflicting statements within them (e.g., Ricoeur's "pulsation" within the Torah which reconciles Jesus' opposition to the traditions of the elders and Matthew's "Jesus" who declares that the last iota of the Law will be fulfilled in the Kingdom).

II

Another feature of the texts which is related to the matter of *historical* investigation is their historical character itself--or, to follow Ricoeur's attractive "polysemic and polyphonic concept of revelation," we might add the "polychronic" concept as well. By this I mean that the pluralism of the Biblical texts is not merely a pluralism of ideas; it is also a historical pluralism. It is not a synchrony of diverse texts, or a collection of synchronous texts, but a growing diachrony of a pluralism which develops dialectically. It is not any longer adequate or even correct to treat *Job*, for example, in the holistic way Ricoeur does (in his section on Wisdom discourse, and as he did in *The Symbolism of Evil* at greater length); while it is important to treat a Biblical text as though it were a single creation of a single mind in order to see aspects of it otherwise missed (a point I have been making repeatedly throughout the past twenty-five years), it is nevertheless also important to treat historically growing texts in terms of the diversity of viewpoints which went into their construction. Job, as treated here, is seen *solely* in terms of the last redactor, whose simple analysis of the problem is already answered by Job in the early stages of the dialogue. If this answer were legitimate, then the *friends* were right, and Job should have shut up long before. The richness of Job is precisely in its powerful demolition of the easy answers offered by the redactor who added the final chapter and by the one who explained it in the late prologue. Is *only* the last supplementer of the text to be heard? *True historical* pluralism will allow the diversity *within* a "book" to sound forth, the debate to continue. And it is characteristic of the Biblical materials that they exhibit this pluralism, and further, endorse it in the main (as I have shown elsewhere).

III

Finally, I must suggest that the New Testament materials do not very readily fit the framework offered by Ricoeur's analysis (in section I), which seems tailor-made for the Old Testament. Even in the Old Testament, we miss the curious form called the Apocalypse, where the author claims visions and revelations of the most direct sort. It is not the same as Prophetic discourse at all, as even a casual reading of Daniel will reveal (as will a reading of Revelation in the New Testament). But when we turn to the New Testament, what we actually find are: (1) Gospels, (2) Acts, (3) Letters, and (4) Apocalypse. Only the one example of (2) is much like the analysis of Ricoeur, for it might be "Narrative discourse." The type in (4) is omitted from even the Old Testament, as just noted. Nothing in Ricoeur's analysis resembles the

Letters or Epistles as modes of revelation. And the Gospels are curious precisely in that they really are *not* narrative discourse, nor are they prophetic discourse, although they contain much narrative and contain prophetic-like utterances of Jesus. Two distinctive features of the Gospels differentiate them into a novel mode of revelatory discourse (as Amos Wilder has shown, in terms other than that of the following analysis):

1. Their revelatory quality is in their witness to the revelation given in the person who is their center and focus, Jesus; it is a considerable intensification of Ricoeur's "history" as the focus of revelation, for here it is not a history, but a man--his actions, his passion, his words, his death--that is presented as God's revelation. Perhaps they can be subsumed under "narrative," but only at the cost of what distinguishes them from all models in the Old Testament.

2. Their form is in fact not that of narrative in the usual sense, but much more that of poetry or poetic writing: they are in some cases sophisticated literary structures, and at least part of what constitutes the revelatory character of the Gospel is found in *parallelism* between *this* structure and some *ancient* structure (e.g., Mark/the Exodus event; Matthew/the Five Books of Torah, plus the book of Joshua-Jesus). The *modeling* utilized by the Evangelists is crucial for them; unless it is included in the "Primary" Expressions of Revelation," the Gospels will not be adequately handled.

All in all, my questions and critique do not so much contradict Ricoeur's essay as ask for its supplementation and its further qualification in the direction of Biblical precision.

Response by Dr. Wendy O'Flaherty,
Visiting Lecturer in History and Phenomenology of Religions
Graduate Theological Union, Berkeley

When Professor Ricoeur remarks that his approach "is limited to cultures
which possess books," he seems to imply that he intends his formulations to
be cross-cultural in scope; he refers specifically to Judaism, Christianity, and
Islam (though all of his examples are from the Old Testament). Moreover, in
his discussion of Wisdom discourses, Professor Ricoeur calls attention to the
Book of Job, which has been the basis of an earlier study which is clearly
intended to be cross-cultural, *The Symbolism of Evil*. This book has recently
come under fire for precisely this intention;[1] yet I have found it an extremely
useful model in my own work on Hindu approaches to the symbolism of evil. The
question thus arises in my mind: is the present essay on revelation truly
cross-cultural?

Several of the basic formulations are highly illuminating when applied
to Indian materials. The concept of scripture as revelation in the broader
sense of the world, as *revealing* "a proposed world," as a vehicle by which God
both reveals and conceals himself, is vividly true of classical Hindu texts,
particularly of mythological texts, and more particularly of Vaiṣṇava
mythological texts: Kṛṣṇa hides in the events of the folk-tale "like fire within
coals" (as the *Bhāgavata Purāṇa* puts it) and bursts out not merely in the obvious
epiphanies (like that in the eleventh canto of the *Bhagavad Gītā*) but in the
veiled hints of the poet throughout the work. Śiva, too, remains implicit,
latent, in his encounters with humankind; only in the scripture is he revealed--
as the god who masquerades as the heretic, the Brahmin in the guise of an
Untouchable.

The definitions of prophetic discourse, narrative discourse, and
prescriptive discourse are also valuable hermeneutic tools for the understanding
of Indian scriptures. The Hindus distinguish sharply between *śruti*, "that which
is heard," inspired texts such as the Vedas, and *smṛti*, "that which is remem-
bered," texts attributed to human sages. Only the first would be regarded as
revelation in the classical sense of the word; but both are clearly revealed in
Ricoeur's definition, the first being prophetic, the second prescriptive.
Indeed, both *śruti* and *smṛti* behave like prophetic discourse in having double
authors, men and gods; the first is dictated by gods and recorded by men, while
the second (as in the case of the *Mahābhārata*, which is said to have been
dictated by the sage Vyāsa to the god Gaṇeśa, acting as Vyāsa's amanuensis) is
dictated by men and recorded by gods. Gods are also regarded as the authors of
narrative discourse, in which, as Ricoeur suggests, the author (and the human
scribe) often disappear and the events recount themselves. The way in which
"the menace announced in the prophecy" breaks into the narrative discourse is
also an important insight into Hindu eschatology, where the text actually
vacillates between past tense and future tense in the description of the Kali
Age and that was/will be.

It is in the realm of the final two categories, Wisdom discourse and
hymnic discourse, and in the subsequent discussions of confession, testimony,
and martyrdom, that the model ceases to be applicable to the Indian materials.
Job's questions are indeed central to the Indian theodicy, but his response
to the events of his experience make no sense at all in the Indian world view;
here, incidentally, is where the *Symbolism of Evil* also diverges from the

potential cross-cultural model. Confession and testimony are irrelevant to Indian theology of the orthodox period (though they play an important part in one branch of Hinduism, the Tamil *bhakti* school, which is a world unto itself). If a scripture of revelation can thrive without these elements, one is left wondering about their *theoretical* centrality even in the Old Testament, however well their *actual* centrality, their historical assumption of a key role in this tradition, may be established.

---

[5]Cf. Laurence L. Alexander, "Ricoeur's *Symbolism of Evil* and Cross-Cultural Comparison," in *Journal of the American Academy of Religion* XLIV (1976) 705-714.

Response by Dr. Kenan B. Osborne, Professor of Theology
President of the Franciscan School of Theology
Graduate Theological Union, Berkeley

The structure of this brief response to Dr. Ricoeur's lecture will
follow the structure of the lecture itself, namely, part one will consider the
topic of originary expressions of revelation and part two the response of a
hermeneutic philosophy.

Part one: To be commended is the polysemic and polyphonic description
of the expression of revelation, which fleshes out the very meaning of
revelation and embodies it in living history and the multiple forms of human
expression, none of which can claim total dominance. The necessarily and
understandably brief survey of the various genres of discourse do, however,
raise questions that might be further probed. In Vatican II, for instance, an
emphasis on God revealing himself, rather than on God revealing a message,
places the ground of all revelation on self-communication, with the result that
the expressions of such self-revelation (by God) place us before an "archaeo-
logy of the subject." This cannot help but involve us with a God who is hidden,
the something secret, the limit-idea of revelation. Nonetheless, self-
communication implies on the part of the one to whom this self-communication
is being made a personal response, in theological terms, faith. It would seem
that it is this self-communication of God--never total, always both manifesting
and at the same time hiding--which is originary and the discourse is secondary.
In other words, there is a primordiality to self-communication/personal response,
which induces the various genres of discourse. However, there is a
dialectical tension between the personal response and the expression, so that
the very attempt to re-read or re-state the response furthers the recognition
of the self which is revealing, a process that moves us toward an "eschatology
of the spirit." What I might have appreciated more is some words by Dr.
Ricoeur on the inter-relationship of revelation and faith. Just as Dr. Ricoeur
has noted that consciousness today needs to be redescribed in terms of the
unconscious and vice-versa, so too, revelation and faith cannot be adequately
treated except in dialectical inter-relationship.

A second area in this first part that would, I hope, be interesting to
pursue is this: in Christian theology, Catholic and Protestant, there is a long-
standing view that it was not what Jesus said nor what he did which is the
heart of his revelation, but that he himself is ultimately the revelation of the
godhead, at least within the structures of our history. Here we neither have
a text nor do we have a literary genre, but a self. This is, of course,
strongly asserted by theologians who see in Jesus the sacrament of one's
encounter with God. I raise this merely as a further point of discussion.

Part two: The key issues here are, of course, the claim of philosophical
discourse to transparent objectivity and subjective autonomy. In the light of
what Dr. Ricoeur has written, would there be an enrichment to the disclaimer of
an autonomous subject were one to enrich the philosophical aspect of the case
with the entire question of *Sein* which Heidegger employs to see the primordiality
of non-autonomy over against any secondary autonomy? I have in mind his statement on the Other: "Thus in characterizing the encountering of Others, one is
again still oriented by that *Dasein* which is in each case one's own. But even
in this characterization does one not start by marking out and isolating the 'I'
so that one must then seek some way of getting over to the Others from that

isolated subject? To avoid this misunderstanding we must notice in what sense we are talking about "the others." By "Others" we do not mean everyone else but me--those over against whom the "I" stands out. They are rather those from whom, for the most part, one does *not* distinguish oneself--those among whom one is too. This Being-there-too (*Auch-da-sein*) with them does not have the ontological character of a Being-present-at-hand-along-"with"-them within a world. This "with" is something of the character of *Dasein*; the "too" means a sameness of Being as circumspectively concernful "Being-in-the-world."

It would seem to me that beyond the question of poetics, which is linguistic, there is an even more philosophical origin for the non-autonomousness of the subject in the question of *Sein*.

As regards the question of transparent objectivity, is there perhaps a way of involving the existential negativity of Tillich's philosophy into the entire gamut of beings and thereby render transparency philosophically impossible, since all beings, though essentially transparent remain within the actuation of existential negativity? Again this is posed merely as a possible enrichment of the thoughts of Dr. Ricoeur.

Response by Dr. Kevin A. Wall, O.P., Professor of Theology and Philosophy
Saint Albert's College, Graduate Theological Union, Berkeley

1. With respect to page 2

   a. There seems to be a two-fold division of the levels, which may or may
      not be identical

      1. lex orandi, lex credendi   1. same
      2. ecclesial dogma   2. same
      3. magisterium   3. theological investigation

      Is this intended and therefore is it the intention of the paper to
      equate theological investigation and magisterium? If not, how does the
      paper intend to distinguish them?

   b. With respect to the affirmation that the second and the third levels
      are derived and subordinate, does that or does it not give them a lower
      value of authority?

   c. With respect to the third level, isn't it precisely here too that a
      difference of *testimony* divides the Christian community and therefore
      is it not the case that

      1. since the paper concedes a quasi-selfinvalidating character to
         testimony, it therefore concedes the right of a portion of the
         Christian community to testify validly that it accepts magisterium;
      2. that therefore Professor Ricoeur's statement on page 2 that "The
         particular amalgamation which I deplore and that I am seeking to
         combat ..." is *itself* a testimony in which he, as a witness,
         " ... may so implicate himself in his testimony that it becomes the
         best proof of his conviction ..." or, in other words, one in which
         he declares himself to be a witness against level 3?

   d. From this point of view, isn't the paper therefore not so much a device
      to combat or defend the acceptance of level 3 but a declaration of faith
      or a testimony which then asks to be analyzed as such, i.e. on its own
      terms?

2. "So instead of having to confront a monolithic concept of revelation, which
   is only obtained by transforming these different forms of discourse into
   propositions ..." page 3.

   a. This seems to say

      1. the transformation of these different forms of discourse into
         propositions is a monolithic concept of revelation;
      2. the transformation is possible since it has occurred;
      3. it is invalid since it makes revelation monolithic in concept.

   b. Are not all of these statements *testimony* in the sense of the paper?

3. Isn't the "one-sided emphasis of Fuchs and Ebeling ..." such with respect to
   a *testimony* which is different from theirs and therefore one in virtue of
   which they cannot be themselves criticized since they cannot be held to render

the same testimony?

4. "First I will reiterate ..." page 11, 12.

    a. Does this say that religious discourse may *legitimately* be transformed to the level of theological assertions such as "God exists," etc. but that its analysis should not *begin* there;

    b. or does it say that theological assertions such as the ones cited are not legitimate explications of the more radical level of religious discourse, such as the paper seems to make its thesis on page 2?

5. As a general question, does the paper propose a radical *reductionism* in modalities of revelation in virtue of which the transformation of these modalities into theological assertions such as the ones given is impossible? And in this respect does the qualification of the "polyphonic and polysemic concept of revelation" as *analogical* mean this?

6. "... in none of its modalities may revelation be included in and dominated by knowledge ..." page 14. But may knowledge be included in and dominated by its modalities such that it is legitimately abstracted from them and as such constitutes level 3 of theological affirmations which are thereby justified?

7. Need language in its poetic function be *identified* with language in its revelatory function (or theological)? Doesn't it suffice to posit an *analogical* unity here as in the modalities of revelation? One would then simply say that revelation uses language in a way which is analogical to the way in which poetry uses it.

MINUTES OF THE COLLOQUY OF 13 FEBRUARY 1977

List of Participants

Professors at the *University of California, Berkeley*
    Robert Bellah (*Sociology*)
    Baruch Bokser (*Near Eastern Studies*)
    Julian Boyd (*English*)
    Walter Burkert (*Sather Professor, Classical Literature*)
    John D. Coolidge (*English and Comparative Literature*)
    Jack R. Lundbom (*Lecturer, Religious Studies*)
    Thomas G. Rosenmeyer (*Classics and Comparative Literature*)
    Wayne Shumaker (*English*)

Professors at the *Graduate Theological Union*
    John L. Bogart (*Continuing Education*)
    Bill Herzog II (*Biblical Studies and Art*)
    Edward C. Hobbs (*Theology and Hermeneutics*)
    Sherman E. Johnson (*Dean and Professor of New Testament, Emeritus*)
    Wendy O'Flaherty (*History and Phenomenology of Religion*)
    Kenan Osborne (*Systematic Theology*)
    Massey H. Shepherd, Jr. (*Liturgics*)
    Kevin Wall (*Systematic Theology and Philosophy*)
    John H. Wright (*Systematic Theology*)
    Wilhelm Wuellner (*New Testament*)

Professor at the *University of Chicago*
    Paul Ricoeur (*Philosophy*)

Professor at *Mills College*
    John Staten (*Religion*)

Professor at *Midland College (Fremont, Nebraska)*
    Erick Egertson (*Religion and Philosophy*)

Professor at *San Francisco State*
    Neil Forsyth (*Lecturer, Comparative Literature, Philosophy, English*)

Professor at the *Mennonite Seminary, Fresno*
    Elmer A. Martens (*Old Testament*)

Stanford University
    Robert Hamerton-Kelly (*Dean of the Chapel*)
    John Martin (*Course Assistant Dean of the Chapel*)

Visiting Scholars, Graduate Theological Union
    Geraldine Kelley (*Early Nineteenth-century Russian Literature*)
    Anitra Bingham Kolenkow (*Jewish Studies, Christian Literature*)

Students at the Graduate Theological Union
    Marvin Brown
    John J. Engeln
    Irene Lawrence (recording secretary)
    Daryl Schmidt
    Lavette Teague

MINUTES OF THE COLLOQUY OF 13 FEBRUARY 1977

THE DISCUSSION*

Wuellner: I asked Professor Ricoeur to identify two or three issues arising from his paper that he would like to see discussed. And I would like those who wrote responses to do the same.

Ricoeur: I was mainly concerned with confronting the philosopher with the question of revelation. This should be emphasized, because the responses tended to isolate the first part from the second, for the sake of the interests of the theologian. But I claim to be doing *philosophy*; the basis of the paper is the philosophical question of how to respond to the concept of revelation. So the first part is not an introduction, but the negative side, contrasting with the second part, the positive, philosophical, side. In the first part I tried to construct the concept of revelation. It is a stumbling block for philosophical reflection when taken as monolithic, as often proposed by theologians. So I tried to propose a more complex, heterogeneous, and polyphonic concept. Therefore, this could be the *first issue: the consistency of the concept of revelation*. Is it only one concept, or is it a bundle of concepts with only analogical links, or family resemblances?

A *second issue* could be *the place of theological discourse in relation to* what I called *the primary expressions of faith*. I think the philosopher should address himself, not to the most refined, speculative, form of discourse, but to the "barbarian" element in Christianity. This relation between the orders of discourse--the primary, the second order, the third order--should be the second issue.

The *third issue* concerns the second part of the paper; it is *the relation between poetics in general and what is specific to religious language*. It is within the framework of a poetics that the philosopher makes sense of the claim of revelation. The last part is a discussion within the framework of continental philosophy. The claim that the subject is the origin of meaning is in the tradition of German Idealism, of Fichte and Husserl. I tried to say that in the context of testimony, the claim has been dropped. The philosopher must first lose his soul--the claim to be the origin of meaning.

Boyd: Professor Ricoeur said at the beginning that philosophers should not talk about their own categories within their own categories. That is true. But unfortunately Anglo-American philosophy followed that advice too well, and looked to linguistics. It was disastrous when Austin dissolved philosophy in the name of linguistics. Searle made that clear, and dropped speech acts. In my "joke" response, I was trying to point out that there is a little Husserl underneath Searle, which has now come out into the open. I would like to talk about that little Husserl--namely, intentionality, and second order intentionality, the sort of discourse analysis in which the modalities are peeled off so there is something like revelation or events which express themselves. This is a version of Professor Ricoeur's second issue.

Hobbs: All of us in one way or another pointed to Professor Ricoeur's emphasis

---

*Summarized by Irene Lawrence.

on the primacy of event in revelation. The place to begin might be the way
in which *event* has a primary focus in his work, rather than *discourse*, which
arises from the event.

O'Flaherty: My question was whether the elements which Professor Ricoeur
sees as part of revelation are necessarily all present all of the time. That
is, what is true of revelation that is not true of other sacred literature?
To identify revelation, are you thinking only in terms of an Old Testament
model? Is that what revelation is, or is it just what the Old Testament is?

Ricoeur: In this paper, I used the Bible as my text, and within this text I
tried to discover a richness of meaning which I thought could not be found in
other kinds of discourse. Pursuing this would bring us to the second stage
of the discussion. But my claim was that a great part of the theology of
revelation has been built on an extrapolation of the prophetic mode, which I
called the "double voice," the voice behind the voice. I tried to use an
aspect of literary criticism concerning the other modes of discourse to open
other possibilities of making sense of revelation. So my problem is not a
reduction, but an increase of meaning.

     It would be a problem of comparative religion to know whether other texts
present the same variety of modes of revelation. But my claim was that each
mode of discourse was not merely a rhetorical device, but conveys its message
precisely because of its mode. For example, in narrative discourse, God is
the one who does things; he is the actor. But in prophetic discourse, he is the
one behind the voice. There are several positions of the word "God."
Therefore I would not say that I am in the line of Austin, but more in the line
of literary criticism, more like rhetoric in the sense of Amos Wilder, when
he speaks of the rhetoric of early Christianity.

Boyd: I really meant Austin to be the "barbarian," who makes one barbaric
speech act, and there is no discourse after that. There is only one performative,
"I hereby prophesy," and everything after that is prophecy. That seems shallow,
and you have deepened it.

Ricoeur: Of those in the linguistic analysis tradition, I would most like to
be associated with Stanley Cavell.[1] He says that language is not about itself,
but about what it says. So I see no conflict between speaking of "event" and
narrative discourse.

Boyd: But later you say that within poetics, language turns back upon itself.
Is that consistent?

Ricoeur: Yes, because the theory of poetic discourse is not about any one kind
of discourse, but is a general function of discourse. I start like Northrop
Frye, that poetic discourse first suspends the reference to ordinary objects, but
only for the sake of opening a second order of reference, that to my existence
in the world. Therefore it is half of the truth that poetic discourse is about
itself. Really, because it *seems* to be about itself, it can suspend ordinary
reference to open up an "extraordinary" reference.

Boyd: That is not the same. If within a Quine-like simplicity there is a first

---

[1]Stanley Cavell, *Must We Mean What We Say?* (New York: Scribners 1969).

order of reference, you say that it is that level of reference that Jakobson talks of that refers back to itself,[2] and that that is naive. Are you saying that there is a second order redescription of reference?

Ricoeur: I got from Jakobson the idea of split reference. He uses this, saying that no discourse is without reference, but that it refers in a new way. This is what may open up a new way to the theological discussion of revelation. It is not a kind of reference about which I may raise questions of verification, but of manifestation. I claim in the second part that in order for language to display this capacity for making reality manifest, it has to lose some ordinary descriptive functions. I call it "second order," but in fact it is the primitive language, which has been overshadowed by "ordinary" language.

Boyd: So you are claiming that what is supposed to be referentially transparent, supposed to be first order, is really second order already, and actually referentially opaque?

Ricoeur: Yes. I have to recapture it because dealing with objects has become my first order language. To speak like Aristotle, what is discovered late is first in ontological· dignity. I want to emphasize that the poetics of the second part is not one kind of discourse among those in the first part, but is the way in which the philosopher has to speak of all kinds of discourse. All discourse with a split reference I call "poetic discourse."

Osborne: In the first part of the paper, Professor Ricoeur spoke of "expressions of revelation"--a very apt phrase--and then gave the genres. Beginning with such a phrase might imply that we know that there is a God out there revealing himself to us through these methods. In other words, one begins by listing the expressions within the Biblical material as to the way in which God has revealed himself to us. But if we leave the God question in brackets for a moment, is there anything within the human construct that would be open to such a possible referent (that we might call God)? How would this work? Your paper seemed to set the answer before the question.

Ricoeur: I put it in terms of claim, not question or answer. There is a claim addressed to me by a certain kind of discourse; there are books raising this claim. There are claims to verification in terms of knowledge, and to autonomy in terms of subjectivity. I tried to put the first claim so that it could not be rejected just because it is falsely presented.

Osborne: But what in the human is open to a claim of God?

Ricoeur: I give two answers in this paper; there are others. First, it is in language. I have other uses of language than the instrumental use, that by which I manipulate objects. Another use is listening in order to receive the meaning of my existence. I call this "poetic." So language is the place in which I am open to something other than my own existence. Second, there is testimony, my own movement to lose a certain claim. The Suffering Servant is the paradigm of what I try to do reflectively. The task of reflection is shown to be contingent; what is necessary in theological terms is historically conditioned.

---

[2]Roman Jakobson, "Linguistics and Poetics," in T. Sebeok (ed.), *Style in Language* (M.I.T. Press 1960).

Osborne: From an agnostic stance, all sorts of claims are made on every individual, some valid and some not. If there is a claim by way of revelation by God, the first question as a philosopher would be, what in a person is open to "God," or "infinite transcendent," or "absolute."

Ricoeur: My strategy was not to start from me, but from the world of a text. And the testimony is the other. So I have to start from the other always, not from me, because I cannot lift a *claim* by looking at it.

Herzog: I would like to pursue Professor Ricoeur's statement concerning how the notion of revelation differs from one mode of discourse to another. To understand the mechanism of *how* they differ, should we ask the question of point of view? In prophetic discourse, the assumption is a coincidence between the divine point of view and the human. The prophet's "I" is "I" and "Yahweh" simultaneously. Point of view is much more complex in narrative discourse. If we bracket for the moment Professor Hobbs's important question of how much this applies to the New Testament, we see Paul struggling over the question of point of view in the epistles--"Paul" or the double voice? In hymnic discourse, the voice speaking is very aware that it is addressing a "thou"--the points of view do not coincide. An analysis of revelation in terms of the range of the two voices might be useful.

Ricoeur: Point of view may not be appropriate to all of them. The hymnic mode is so often forgotten in discussion. What constitutes the revelatory event is the *Aufhebung* of fear and passions, the transmutation of feelings. It does not have the quality of an event. Is there a point of view here besides story-telling? In fiction, the question of point of view is linked with the narrative element. One could argue that the point of view is masked and unmasked in the different modes, and that might be a means by which one could understand *how* revelation differs from one mode of revelation to another.

Lundbom: Professor Ricoeur's categories are very good, but are they, perhaps, a bit too neat? For example, Jeremiah is used as an example of prophetic discourse. There is to be sure the voice behind the voice, but we also have in Jeremiah prophetic confessions which are similar to the hymnic mode in which the human voice of the prophet converses with God. So, in Jeremiah at least, it is not always that clear-cut.

Hobbs: Professor Ricoeur did not mean that the *whole book* with the prophet's name is solely in the prophetic mode. There would be different modes from passage to passage.

Egertson: Some passages of Jeremiah, for example, would be classified as hymnic discourse.

Ricoeur: The prophetic genre is a collection of genres, but I am not defining genres.

Kolenkow: Professor Ricoeur talked about moving beyond prophecy as a category, saying positive things about the other categories. Is this positiveness a consequence of what seems a kind of threat in the double voice, or a menace of the forecast of the end time, perhaps inherent in the prophetic stance? The other categories are not so threatening.

Ricoeur: Because one dimension of the concept of revelation has been over-emphasized and frozen, we think that inspiration is the only, the univocal, concept of revelation. It is something whispering in the ear, the Gospels being dictated. This is a reification, a reduction of something much richer. Only one book is called "Revelation." So I wanted to modulate the concept, to make it more polysemic. The danger is to make it too scattered. Is my notion of analogy a kind of flight from this difficulty? I find myself and the Scholastics working between synonymy and mere homonomy. Sometimes analogy is a mere trick, but sometimes it is a good tool for thinking in between these two things. Wittgenstein meets this problem with the concept of family resemblances.

Hobbs: Since Professor Ricoeur especially wants to undermine the view of revelation as dictation, might it not be worthwhile to make a distinction between *canon* and *revelation*? Scripture does not make the claim that it is all revelation. The community claimed that it is all the *measure* ("canon") of revelation, that revelation is congruent with it. "God's mark is in history before being in speech; it is only secondarily in speech, inasmuch as the history is brought to language." Perhaps then revelation should not have been identified with all these modes of discourse; instead, these modes point to something more primary than themselves.

Ricoeur: I have the notion from Fackenheim of history-making events. Of course, we do not deal with all events, but with some decisive events, which have a founding function for the community--the Exodus event, the Resurrection event.

Hobbs: If that is carried further, the variety of modes would be secondary. The founding events are the Exodus and Jesus. If revelation is found *there*, then the various modes of discourse in the canon *interpret* them, *respond* to them. The question of which of these are the voice of God becomes almost meaningless, because none of them are, not even the prophet who says "I." A constant issue in the Old Testament is whether or not the prophet speaks truth. That is discovered through what takes place in history.

Ricoeur: I wondered about the convertibility of one mode of discourse to another, such as a parable becoming a proverb. A narrative has also a prescriptive element; because the Exodus is linked to Sinai, narrative is linked to law. In other cases, the relation may be opposition. The prophet's threat shatters confidence linked to the past; the discourses cancel. What is new appears through the threat addressed to what is confessed in the narrative. Many kinds of relationships should be studied besides mere juxtaposition of modes.

Shumaker: There is a remarkable similarity between Biblical prophecy and some denunciatory satire, say, Juvenal. Such satirists may appeal to the wrath of the gods; are they also prophets?

Kolenkow: Satire is mockery, but prophecy has something else. Satire does not necessarily claim to have God behind it.

Shumaker: Roman satire is basically attack, not mockery. And the gods can be invoked, and their impending vengeance announced.

Shepherd: Is the testimony of the mystic subsumed in the categories Professor

Ricoeur has described? There are some hints of it in Scripture, although most mystical experience is described in later literature. It is essentially an ineffable experience, yet there is the attempt to describe it. Is it narrative?

Ricoeur: As the end of the classifications, I put outside a category the relation between revelation and its contrary, the God who withdraws, the relation of the revealed and the hidden. I linked that to the burning bush. Perhaps this is the origin of a fundamental correlation in language--the analogical and the negative. On the one side in language there are metaphorical approximations about God, and on the other, the denial of all categorization. A mystical vision seems not to belong to the Biblical mode; it is more Neo-Platonic.

Shepherd: An Old Testament example would be Isaiah's vision. And Paul refers to ineffable experiences.

Wuellner: He calls them ἄρρητα ῥήματα (2 Cor 12:4).

Shepherd: I thought that this element of the revealed and the hidden characterized all your categories. Would the testimony of the mystic be a way of bringing them together in a uniform category?

Ricoeur: I suspect it is not specifically Biblical.

Shepherd: The book of Revelation comes close to the mystic report. It was a vision in the state of ecstasy.

Ricoeur: But the dreams and visions are put in the form of narrative. The mode of confession is autobiographical narrative. Narrative brings the mystical experience within language.

Hamerton-Kelly: The world I live in believes that once someone is categorized as a theologian, he or she can be effectively ignored. Yet Professor Ricoeur's work is extraordinarily influential in that world. So is he a theologian or a philosopher? He took Biblical revelation seriously and explained to us and the world how effective a way it is of allowing God to approach us. I was strongly reminded of the theology of Karl Barth, particularly in the relationship of the event and the text. Now, is this strictly a philosophical exercise, interpreting the phenomena of orthodox Protestantism, or do you yourself make theological commitments?

Ricoeur: The position of theological discourse is not so well presented in this paper, because I had been reading many things about revelation by theologians, and in direct consequence I took a more negative stand than usual. I think there is a specific task of doing theology, and the other orders of discourse are all important. For example, only at the level of the second order, the confession of the community, can I answer the question of canon. A text makes sense when the community interprets it. The third order is not the task of the community, but of the intellectuals and academics, to do theology. They put in a rational framework the scattered elements of preaching. The function of theology is to critique preaching. But this presupposes the creedal discourse of the community. I do not want to mix levels. It is because theological discourse has been confused with the creeds that we have *rabies theologica*. Theology needs to be deemphasized in terms of the community, and emphasized in terms of personal and intellectual integrity, to understand what

one believes. Theology is always composite; it borrows from existing philosophical categories; it is mixed discourse. This is not my task. The
theologian's question is how to criticize preaching in a coherent order. The
philosopher tries to approximate with his own categories what is external
to his discourse but basic to his life.

Staten: I see a subordination of discourse concerning God as creator to that
concerning God as savior. Where in primary, Biblical discourse is the grounding
of secondary level discourse, such as "I believe in God, maker of heaven and
earth?"

Ricoeur: In the Wisdom literature. It is not late literature, although we
tend to link it with certain kinds of books. But the problem of creation is
already Wisdom, because it is an attempt to understand how one can belong to a
good creation and a wicked history. The creation story adjusts the old
mythological world to the confession of faith implied in the narrative. (Here
I follow von Rad.) Around the nucleus of the Exodus (the constitution of the
people), those suspicious, dangerous myths could be recovered as a preface,
could be historicized. But Wisdom is not the predominant mode of the Old
Testament; narrative is, within which we speak of a God who does something with
his people, so it is fundamentally historical, unlike the Greek Gods of the
cosmos.

Staten: Would you connect this with that part of your paper in which you deal
with Nabert? For him also, primary affirmation comes out of the problem of evil.

Wright: I was impressed by the way in which the claims of revelation are
mediated to us through language, through the world of the text. But what
characterizes the event of revelation as revelatory? Are all events revelatory
to one who sees, or only certain ones?

Ricoeur: Within a narrative, it is the capacity of an event to found a
tradition, a community, which then confesses the event as the origin of its
existence.

Wright : The community recognizes the event as constituting itself, and
therefore it becomes revelatory?

Ricoeur: I do not want to press the "therefore." It is the same movement,
circular, like all good things.

Wright: The Declaration of Independence founded us. It is political, but there
are theological overtones. Still, I would hesitate to call it "revelatory."

Ricoeur: It is the conjunction of all these modes of discourse which display
the dimension I called "poetics," and that proposes a world in which I can
dwell. The whole structure--not just *this* event--functions poetically in my
life and radiates its revelatory function from one genre to another.

Wuellner: Then every culture, every community can claim such revelatory
events.

Hobbs: That seems self-evident, unless one claims that only one is true. Even
within one community, Israel, the struggle goes on as to whether the Exodus is

constitutive, the revelation of Yahweh's act. What constitutes liberation, or who is the true prophet? What are the constitutive events, and what god is revealed in them? As resolution takes place, a certain community comes into being.

Wall: Then one should not make so sharp a distinction between *the* event and the expression of it. It is not the event which constitutes the revelation, and secondarily the speaking of it, but the speaking of the event which constitutes the revelation. To come down strongly on the side of poetry is to come down on the side of making and giving sense to modes of listening for revelation, as well as modes of passivity.

Ricoeur: I do not want these to be alternatives, either discourse *or* the event. This is the structure of reference, that genuine narrative discourse effaces itself for the sake of the event that is brought to language. There is a mutual foundation for discourse and event; they belong together. Carnap puts it well when he speaks of the *wirkungsgeschichtliches Bewusstsein*, the awareness of language belonging to the event it retells. The teller belongs to his own history.

Wall: In the writing, the thing narrated takes over from the narrator. You do not mean that the revelation is a giving of meaning by an individual, but the thing revealed also takes over.

Hobbs: In fact, Professor Ricoeur says on p. 10, "Truth no longer means verification, but manifestation; that is, letting what shows itself, be."

Boyd: The main difficulties are the concepts "event" and "truth." Event in history and narration in the past can be "true." But if prophecy in its central sense is not prediction but the interpretation of God's will, then if what God wills comes to be, it does not become "true," but it becomes "fulfilled." If "fulfill" is the major word, it is beyond truth. Truth, in fact, fulfills truth conditions. Therefore primary reason, as you say, has something to do with will, and if it is God's will, it is not the threatening will Dr. Kolenkow was concerned about. "Fulfillment" is in the Wisdom literature, and it is Aristotle's "happiness."

Bokser: The works of Abraham Joshua Heschel focus on the same two things with which Professor Ricoeur deals. *The Theology of Ancient Israel*[3] is a study of rabbinic thought especially as to the meaning and definition of revelation. It tries to demonstrate a non-literal interpretation of revelation and Biblical narrative. His other works try to respond to the philosophical critic of religion and "God-talk." It likewise employs the language of poetry to convey the ineffable.

Professor Ricoeur rightly says that the philosophical definition of religion is incorrect; there is more to religion. The problem relates to us as academics. We try--but inevitably cannot succeed--to convey to students an experience of the divine or religion. We might try poetry to convey it. But ultimately what we describe in terms of verifiability remains not "meaningful." While we want to be philosophically legitimate, we do not accept philosophy's rules. Would we come up with something philosophically "meaningful" if we change

[3]Two volumes (London and New York 1962, 1965).

the rules as we go along? I believe not. Philosophers will not accept that.

Ricoeur: To put it in terms of Hegelian philosophy: Hegel said that religion is the same as philosophy, except that religion works with symbolic, historical terms (*Vorstellung*), but philosophy uses concepts (*Begriff*). While philosophy is enriched by the imaginative language, eventually the concept overcomes the *Vorstellung*. I would say we have to do with an open language: we are always conceptualizing, especially as philosophers, but we cannot close the gate. We cannot accept from Hegel the idea of absolute knowledge, overcoming the *Vorstellung*. Revelation is that I receive meaning, but I cannot construe meaning. I see the philosopher and the believer in an endless conflict.

Wuellner: I see it in the legacy of Greece: from μῦθος to λόγος.

Ricoeur: The dream of having a pure Biblical theology without a mixture of Greece and others is impossible, because we have to think in the categories which are available to us. We have to find our way between mere juxtaposition and a systematic connection, so the relation between *Vorstellung* and *Begriff* is for me the key. We have to think conceptually.

Osborne: We have been discussing the event itself and the more systematic language in which we might express it. Scholasticism has the question of analogy between the things of this world and the things of the transcendent, divine world. Perhaps as a start, analogy could be restricted, to help explain that what theologians would systematize is analogous--not to God, or to the transcendent world--but to what events are all about. What happens in history, or event, or a believing community, are so many dimensions of this, and then afterwards a theologian or a philosopher puts together a systematic exposition. All we want to say is that there is an analogous relationship between what Hegel, for example, would say, and what Fichte, Aquinas, or Barth would say. I think this would help because it leaves a certain relativity or changeableness to the position of the philosopher or theologian, and gives a certain primordialness to the event.

Ricoeur: I would prefer "approximation" to "analogy." Analogy contains, among other things, the notion of proportionality. I consider my philosophical task to attempt to approximate with my philosophical resources what I receive through another, non-philosophical language, through the polyphony of all non-speculative language, but without ever suppressing the differences. So I never say I can deduce the revelatory claim of the Biblical text from the poetic function in general, although I can approximate what is meant by the claim because I can find something analogous.

Osborne: Would you have, then, some principles of verification, to say which expressions approximate more or less closely?

Ricoeur: The language of verification belongs to one sphere of discourse, and I cannot apply it to another. It is a function of phenomenology to say that there are different regions of objects displaying different claims. The notion of verification belongs to one kind of object, the empirical. But if poetic language is a certain suspension of this referential claim, then the new sphere of reference opened up by this discourse is not susceptible to the question of verification. So to raise the question of verification to the whole of discourse is to judge the whole of discourse according to a part of it. Perhaps it is a part of the idea of "proving" God.

Osborne: I did not mean proof. Even poetic language or artistic expression still claims to approximate, more or less closely. Some things are mere doggerel, not poetry at all. Some things are good music, others are poor. We make value decisions in the question of approximation.

Hobbs: But we would not talk of "verifying" better or worse music.

Kolenkow: The question is how to judge a good piece of art.

Osborne: Yes. And how do we judge good philosophy, or good theology?

Hobbs: "Evaluation" might be better than "verification."

Ricoeur: This involves the question of taste.

Osborne: Perhaps I am reaching over into that. But if you use approximation, there must be some way of saying "this approximates." What is the basis for that? It could be cultural.

Ricoeur: A commitment must make sense in as many sections of life as possible: in relation to suffering, justice, loneliness, etc. There is a network of criteria, or, better, of "signals of quality." Between arbitrariness and veri-fication there is something--this sense of quality, perhaps taste, of what makes sense of as many instances of life as possible.

Kolenkow: We talk of the relation of the narrator to the event. Perhaps there is also the relation to ritual or myth. The society responds to the narrator's story using ritual as a basis for its judgment; if the story corresponds to the ritual or myth and speaks to the society, the society will accept it. This might establish a criterion.

Ricoeur: It is more a commitment than a criterion. We use "criterion" in the situation of a judge weighing claims, but this is a situation in which something has already been destroyed: the fact that I belong to the process which has its revelatory dimension. When I take the position of a judge, I have already transformed the game. I raised the question about the situation which has been distorted by this shift in the subject-object relationship.

Shumaker: Would you say a little more about the "signal of quality" in philosophy? I take it than an old-fashioned criterion like coherence or self-consistency is not satisfactory. It sounds as if the difference between good and bad philosophy is that good philosophy is emotionally satisfying, because it helps us to live with loneliness.

Ricoeur: I applied this to poetry, not philosophy. I agree that philosophy is systematic and coherent, and elaborates its categories and uses them correctly in good arguments. I would not apply the question of "signals of quality" to philosophy.

Bellah: I am a little uncomfortable with moving the discussion so much to aesthetics, however powerful the idea of poetry is here. Serious poetry still raises questions of truth and falsehood, though not perhaps in the verificational sense. I would hope that the discussion of revelation would not abandon some notion of truth.

Brown: I would like to bring this discussion of evaluation back to the paper and the question of testimony. The Bible is called the Old and New *Testaments*. What makes testimony valid? George Campbell's *The Philosophy of Rhetoric* dealt with that in the eighteenth century. One question is what makes testimony persuasive? There are other categories of evaluation as to credibility than those in philosophy and aesthetics. In terms of the validity of the prophets, the most important people were the editors. Deuteronomic editors in exile decided that Jeremiah was the true prophet, and other contemporary prophets were false. So the canon seems very important. The editors, as members of the community, were persuaded that certain testimony was true, and therefore placed these testimonies in what became the canon. One can turn to rhetoric to look at the problem of testimony.

Ricoeur: Are you saying that the last redactors decide who were the true prophets? Rather, it is circular. Closing the canon is an act of the community, but at the same time, the community recognizes what is consistent with its own existence, what founds it.

Brown: It seems to me that there is a certain priority in terms of inclusion in the canon. For example, in early Jewish hermeneutics, the prophets were seen as commentators upon the Torah. The Torah, or Exodus tradition, was primary.

Ricoeur: It is like an arbitrary act which became a kind of faith for the whole community, which henceforth is constituted by this closing of the canon.

Brown: The canon went through various stages; there was a general acceptance of certain books at different periods.

Wuellner: Is canonization in the Judeo-Christian tradition the same process as in the Greek tradition, when in due course some literature became "classical"?

Bokser: If something was deposited in the temple, it became an official document.

Kolenkow: It is not only what the editors included that became the canon, because there were later corrections, to make things fit.

Brown: Closing the canon is a very important hermeneutical process, which is answering the contemporary situation of the Jewish nation in exile. The community-- the audience--is essential.

Kolenkow: This implies that there already was a kind of canon.

Brown: Yes, some oral tradition and some written.

Herzog: If we move towards poetics, are we abandoning (or making secondary) the question of truth and falsehood?

Bellah: It is not a necessary contradiction, but we did seem to be getting very aesthetic.

Herzog: Professor Ricoeur's paper seems to suggest, at least at one point, a common way to understand revelation in terms of its poetic formulation. That would be a sense of the adequacy of vision, or of the rightness of the manifesta- tion of the world which comes through the work as one in which we can live, whether in a narrative or in a systematics. There seems a basis here for judging, for making commitments, to a testimony.

Ricoeur: A verificationist's criterion and the kind of truth implied by these texts differ greatly. Russell says that propositions must have atomic truth, and we can expand them by means of proofs and implications. A proposition can be isolated, and then we can raise the question of verification. Whereas here, we have a system of convergence, not only between different modes of discourse, but different modes of life, of the capacity to make sense of the contradictions of existence, of living together. It is a notion of truth which is contextual, a system of mutually overlapping contexts, reinforcing each other. Therefore one cannot locate the truth claim in one particular place. It is the mutual fitness, the mutual reinforcement of partial criteria which constitute as a whole a truth claim. This is quite different from the notion of logical extension which proceeds from the atomic proposition. Here, the element of self-commitment cannot be excluded. In a sense, it is a wager: I risk my life on this whole and belong to it by this commitment, and I may win or lose.

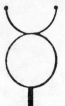

CENTER FOR HERMENEUTICAL STUDIES

in HELLENISTIC and MODERN CULTURE

Graduate Theological Union
University of California

2465 *LeConte Avenue*
Berkeley, CA 94709

$4.00 each, postpaid

* NB: #1, 2, 4, 8, 10, 16, 20, 21 are <u>sold out</u>
and unavailable except in complete sets
of #1-25, @ $100, pp.

Make checks payable to:
Center for Hermeneutical Studies

W. Wuellner, Editor
Protocol Series of the Colloquies of the Center

ISSN 0098-0900

---

*1. *First Century A.D. Literary Culture and Early Christian Literature.* [29 p.]
     Willem Van Unnik (Utrecht), 25 April 1970. LC 75-44025   ISBN 0-89242-000-6

*2. *Paul's Apology II Corinthians 10-13 and the Socratic Tradition.* [30 p.]
     Hans Dieter Betz (Claremont), 5 December 1970. LC 75-35038   ISBN 0-89242-001-4

 3. *Jewish Gnostic Nag Hammadi Texts.* [28 p.]
     James M. Robinson (Claremont), 22 May 1972. LC 75-44331   ISBN 0-89242-002-2

*4. *The Records of Jesus in the Light of Ancient Accounts of Revered Men.* [32 p.]
     Dieter Georgi (Harvard), 21 January 1973. LC 75-35039   ISBN 0-89242-003-0

 5. *The Thunder: Perfect Mind (Nag Hammadi Codex VI, Tractate 2).* [36 p.]
     George MacRae, S.J. (Harvard), 11 March 1973. LC 75-44028   ISBN 0-89242-004-9

 6   *The Aretalogy Used by Mark.* [53 p.]
     Morton Smith (Columbia), 12 April 1973. LC 75-34344   ISBN 0-89242-005-7

 7. *Virgil's Fourth Eclogue.* [45 p.] LC 75-34342
     Gordon Williams, Sather Professor (St. Andrews), 28 May 1973 ISBN 0-89242-006-5

*8. *The Pauline Basis of the Concept of Scriptural Form in Irenaeus.* [59 p.]
     John S. Coolidge (Berkeley), 4 November 1973. LC 75-34343   ISBN 0-89242-007-3

 9. *The Cults of the Epic Heroes and the Evidence of Epic Poetry.* [33 p.]
     Phillip Damon (Berkeley), 27 January 1974. LC 75-24152   ISBN 0-89242-008-1

*10. *Greek and Christian Concepts of Justice.* [72 p.] LC 75-24153
     Albrecht Dihle, Sather Professor (Cologne), 24 February 1974 ISBN 0-89242-009-X

 11. *Narrative Structures in the Book of Judith.* [72 p.]
     Luis Alonso-Schökel, S.J. (Rome), 17 March 1974.LC 75-24155 ISBN 0-89242-010-3

 12. *Aretalogies, Hellenistic "Lives," and the Sources of Mark.* [50 p.]
     Howard C. Kee (Bryn Mawr), 8 December 1974. LC 75-35043   ISBN 0-89242-011-1

 13. *The Idea of Conscience in Philo of Alexandria.* [47 p.] LC 75-35044
     Richard T. Wallis (University of Oklahoma), 12 January 1975 ISBN 0-89242-012-X

 14. *A Social Context to the Religious Crisis of the Third Century A.D.* [52 p.]
     Peter R. L. Brown (Oxford), 9 February 1975. LC 75-38688   ISBN 0-89242-013-8

15. *"General Education" in Philo of Alexandria* [44 p.]
    Thomas Conley (Berkeley), 9 March 1975. LC 75-34413   ISBN 0-89242-014-6

* 16. *The Transcendence of God in Philo: Some Possible Sources.* [44 p.]
    John M. Dillon (Berkeley), 20 April 1975. LC 75-38047   ISBN 0-89242-015-4

17. *Philosophical Hermeneutics and Theological Hermeneutics:*
    Ideology, Utopia, and Faith. [56 p.]   LC 76-13209
    Paul Ricoeur (Paris and Chicago), 4 November 1975   ISBN 0-89242-016-2

18. *Longer Mark: Forgery, Interpolation, or Old Tradition?* [73 p.] LC 76-12558
    Reginald H. Fuller (Alexandria, Va.), 7 December 1975   ISBN 0-89242-017-0

19. *Literary Fashions and the Transmission of Texts in the*
    Graeco-Roman World. [51 p.]
    George D. Kilpatrick (Oxford), 11 January 1976. LC 76-26182 ISBN 0-89242-018-9

* 20. *Freedom and Determinism in Philo of Alexandria.* [35 p.]
    David Winston (Berkeley), 8 February 1976. LC 76-28773   ISBN 0-89242-019-7

* 21. *The Deification of Alexander the Great.* [75 p.] LC 76-29614
    Ernst Badian, Sather Professor (Harvard), 7 March 1976   ISBN 0-89242-020-0

22. *Diatribe in Ancient Rhetorical Theory.* [75 p.] LC 76-28736 ISBN 0-89242-021-9
    George L. Kustas (State University of New York, Buffalo), 25 April 1976

23. *The Use of Stoic Terminology in Philo's Quod Deus Immutabilis*
    Sit 33-50. [46 p.]
    John M. Rist (Toronto), 16 May 1976. LC 76-41275   ISBN 0-89242-022-7

24. *Art as a Hermeneutic of Narrative.* [56 p.] LC 77-4346
    John W. Dixon, Jr. (University of North Carolina, Chapel Hill)
    14 November 1976   ISBN 0-89242-023-5

25. *The Hero Pattern and the Life of Jesus.* [98 p.] LC 77-4835
    Alan Dundes (Berkeley) 12 December 1976   ISBN 0-89242-024-3

26. *Paul's Concept of Freedom in the Context of Hellenistic*
    Discussions about Possibilities of Human Freedom.   [51 p.]
    Hans Dieter Betz (Claremont) 9 January 1977.   ISBN 0-89242-025-1

27. *Hermeneutic of the Idea of Revelation.* [36 p.]
    Paul Ricoeur (Paris and Chicago, 13 February 1977   ISBN 0-89242-026-X

28. *Orphism and Bacchic Mysteries: New Evidence and Old Problems*
    of Interpretation. [48 p.]
    Walter Burkert, Sather Professor (Zurich), 13 March 1977   ISBN 0-89242-027-8

29. *Philo and the Gnostics on Man and Salvation.* [in preparation]
    Birger A. Pearson (Santa Barbara), 17 April 1977   ISBN 0-89242-028-6

30. *Philo's Description of Jewish Practices* [in preparation]
     Baruch Bokser (Berkeley), 5 June 1977   ISBN 0-89242-

Cataloging in Publication
A Program of the Library of Congress Processing Department

All Publications of the Center for Hermeneutical Studies
are available through this Program